PROSPERITY
begins at home...
in **YOUR** own mind

From **YOUR** mind to the world

DOROTHY MANGELSEN

Copyright © 2019 by Dorothy Mangelsen.

ISBN Softcover   978-1-950580-51-4

All rights reserved. No part of this book may be reproduced or transmitted in any form or by any means, electronic or mechanical, including photocopying, recording, or by any information storage and retrieval system without express written permission from the author, except in the case of brief quotations embodied in critical reviews and certain other non-commercial uses permitted by copyright law.

Printed in the United States of America.

To order additional copies of this book, contact:
Bookwhip
1-855-339-3589
https://www.bookwhip.com

This book is dedicated to my family,

Sons

Gary, Richard, Darin

Daughters

Sylvia, Heather.

And my many grandchildren and great grandchildren

My thanks to my special friend

Pauline Krygsman,

who encouraged me to write this book.

I also want to thank my daughter Sylvia.

Without her knowledge and willingness to help me;

I would not have been able to put this book together.

Dorothy Mangelsen

Good day friends; my name is Dorothy.

Before we begin this journey together, let me tell you some things about myself.

I was born in a small town in Canada in 1929. My parents were Catholic and in keeping with the Catholic tradition, I was baptized at the age of about five to ten days old. I was told by my mother, on that day she did not have a name for me, so I was named after three Nuns. In later years, I found out (from my older sibling) I was in fact named after three of the ladies in the neighbourhood.

My mother told me in later years her plan was to abort me; (because, as she told me, she did not want me) but after the Doctor told her what some of the consequences could be he changed her mind. I was the youngest of seven children. My dad passed away when I was four years old (the result of the war)

This put me on the wrong side of the tracks at birth and from then on, life was a very hard uphill climb for me.

My mother kept an old war revolver of my dad's and threatened us many times that she was going to kill us. When I was about ten years of age I broke a blister on my finger with a straight pin, and developed blood poisoning overnight. I awoke with a red line going up my arm. The doctor was called, (I don't know by whom), and he left some purple pills to soak my hand in to bring down the poison. His instructions were 'Don't let the children get these as they are very poisonous.' From that day on, my brother and sister (we were very close as there was very little age difference) had to look through our food every meal to make sure she was not going to put the pills in our food, which she had threatened to do.

My sister and I shared a very small bedroom, and at night, out of fear, we would push the dressing table in front of the door, so she could not get in and kill us in our sleep.

As you can well understand, it was a very very hard life… many years of going without and struggle.

I married at age 20 and had four wonderful children, and one more we adopted, making it five, only to have the marriage end after 25 years, due to his wandering foot and the many insecurities and problems I must have brought with me.

You see, I never heard those three little words from my mother ' I love you' my entire life. So in reality, when I heard them from my ex-husband, they did not mean much either. So, I grew up pretty much a loner.

I want to share one more story with you. If we (myself, my brother and sister) were "bad" we were sent to Sunday school, and as further punishment we also had to stay for junior meeting, so we learned at a very young age that God was a punisher of "bad" children; which in turn made us afraid of dying, and afraid of living. Like the old song said "Lord, this time you gave me a mountain, a mountain that I will never climb".

But, climb it I did. And I will share with you how in this book.

By the time I was in my 60's or 70's, my life started to change. I came across a TV show "Finding the Still Point" narrated by Tom Harper (a former Anglican priest). I also bought his book, which I still have today. I became so interested in finding out about life; I took a course on Therapeutic Touch (laying on of hands, using your energy for good)

I knew there had to be more to life and to this God, other then what I had learned in childhood. There had to be something better for myself and for all of us, besides birth, working and then death.

I became very interested in how our mind works and exactly what we can be, do, and have. I now have a very large collection of books on self-help that I read all the time.

I want to interject one more item from my past in here. I only attended secondary school for two weeks, as I quit school at the age of 16. You see, I had to wear the same skirt and sweater every day, I had no other clothes. Can you imagine my embarrassment as a teenager? And the ridicule I faced every day!

I went all the way through public school not knowing the basics, such as my times tables. Remember, these were the days before computers or calculators. Life was a very hard struggle when you had nothing.

But, out of all the struggles and the readings, came the knowledge that we are creating our own lives with our thoughts. Everything we think comes back, that is how the world keeps revolving and evolving.

Jesus said, "If thou canst believe, all things are possible to him that believeth." (Mark 9:23)

The Universe is the one mind, and we are the thinkers in that one mind, every thought we have is vibrated back to us as a fact. The master 'Jesus' said "as a man thinketh; so shall he be". (Proverbs 23:7)

It took much reading for me to be able to understand this scenario. Life is not 'whatever will be, will be' at all.

We have a conscious mind whose only job is to be right. We have a subconscious mind, whose only job is to prove the conscious mind right. You must guard your every thought and put out only the things you want to come to pass.

If someone had taught me this as a child, I would have created a different, better life for myself. You must keep telling yourself, I am whole, perfect, strong, powerful, loving, harmonious and happy. Speak only the things you want, not what you don't want.

If it is money you desire, do not dwell on lack. If it is health you want, do not dwell on sickness. Whatever you are dwelling on is exactly what you are getting. In trying to bring money into my life, I tried tithing, thinking this what I had to do. It didn't work for me. It's the same as planting seeds, for every seed you sow, there comes a great harvest. So whatever seed you plant, in your conscious mind, the subconscious mind will prove it to true. The real trick to it all is that you must believe it, not just with words, but with your whole being.

All the power for everything and anything you ever wanted is in your mind. You must state clearly what you want, and when you expect the harvest. But you must be realistic, don't ask for a Cadillac, if you only have a Volkswagen faith.

Wealthy people cannot think poor, so they never are. At the same time poor people cannot think rich which is why they stay poor. You must train your mind to start thinking rich, until you believe it…then it will happen. It's the 'Law of Attraction'; it is a universal law that cannot ever be changed. You must only ask for what you want (once) and then start saying thank you, Jesus said "whatever you ask, when you pray (and believe) you shall have it." (Matthew 21:22) Asking is our way of praying.

Please do not get me wrong, I am not telling you not to tithe; it does work for some people. You must sow seed into good ground. Make sure your mind is always good fertile ground before you plant your seed. Then water it well with the water of thanks and faith, and wait for your harvest.

The 'Magic of Believing'* is a marvelous book to read, along with any or all of Dr. Wayne Dyers books. There is also a wonderful little book called T.N.T. I also highly recommend Mike Dooley's books along with Ester & Jerry Hicks and Charles Hanel. All are great, really great self-help books. One of my favourite authors is Earl Nightingale, I really have learned a lot from his books and C.D.'s. I highly recommend all these books if you are serious about changing your life.

But to change your life; you must first change your thoughts. Bring them in line with what you want, not what you don't want.

You need to acquire a burning desire for what you want. Let me explain. I had a desire to have a treadmill, because in the winter it can be dangerous to try to go for walks, this desire has been with me for several months. About one month ago, I went into a store of a friend who deals in used and new furniture. I saw this beautiful treadmill. I asked the price, he said he wanted $500.00. He originally bought it for himself, only to find out he had no room for it. So…I got my treadmill. That is a desire.

An example of a <u>burning</u> desire, sometime last summer I had a craving for a donut. For about three or four days I carried this craving around with me, I know what you are thinking, 'why not go and buy a donut?' I did not want to because of the calories I would consume. So I kept on craving a donut. On about the fourth day my grandson (whom I had not told about my donut craving) walked into the house and handed me a small bag and said "here you go gramma, I bought you a donut, no coffee…just a donut." That is a burning desire. Can you see the difference?

I had a friend who was in desperate need of $50.00. She later told me that for days she was thinking how badly she needed the $50.00. At the same time (not knowing this) I was overtaken with a desire to give her $50.00, I do not know why. When I gave her the money, I said 'I don't know why I am giving this to you; I just felt a need to.' She cried and told me her story. 'Law of Attraction in action' (burning desire)

Another time that same friend needed $20.00. I did not have it at that time. I went uptown into a store, and lo and behold there was a $20 bill lying on the floor, with three other people around, no one picked it up. It was as if they were leaving it for me, I picked it up and took it to my friend. 'Law of Attraction.' My friend was living on a very small pension.

Another time, I had broken a small flower pot; I had in a holder filled with flowers. It was an odd sized flower pot, so obviously I was unable to find a replacement. As I was walking uptown, something told me to look in the gutter. What do you think I found? You are right, the exact size of flower pot I needed, 'Law of Attraction.'

Yet another time I needed $220.00 for something, a few days later my son and daughter-in-law came to visit and for no reason gave me $240.00. My daughter-in-law said ' just to spend' also at the same time, my grandson (who was looking for work and not finding any) was visiting and they gave him $500.00. 'Law of Attraction.'

You may have to start small, manifesting things like a parking spot, a cup of coffee, a phone call, anything, please start someplace.

I had a small house I needed to sell quickly. A couple came along, moved in with a rent to own agreement. With this agreement, I make more money than selling it outright. 'Law of Attraction.'

I am telling you all this to get you strongly motivated, to get a burning desire to change your life for the better. Try one thing at a time, because you can have too many irons in the fire at one time and they burn out quickly.

Anything you have a burning desire for will come to pass. You alone carry the power in you to manifest your desires.

I have read in a lot of my books that you must believe and have the feeling that you already have what you are asking for. It is my own personal belief that if you believe, you already have it, and then you no longer have your burning desire.

I believe it is your burning desire that triggers 'Law of Attraction.' The power is yours to use and remember; if you think you can or if you think you can't either way you are right.

I just returned from shopping. I was talking to a friend of mine, (who works in a grocery store), his words were ' I am fed up with this' we all need to get 'fed up' with things the way they are; now you are ready to change your life.

My intention in writing this book is to motivate you, the reader, to get that burning desire and start changing your life and the world. When you change yourself you change the world.

All the dreamers that have ever lived had a burning desire. Where would we all be and where would our planet be without the dreamer. No doubt, a barren land with no houses, cars, T.V's, radios, dishes, pots & pans, no computers…the list goes on and on. Just use your imagination, be a dreamer if you will, start creating, you can do it.

Read the mantra at the end of this book and that my three year old great- grandson Noah is learning.

Keep telling yourself, I can be, do and have anything I want. For instance, in my case, at the age of 84, I had my first book of children's poems published, (A Book of Children's Poems by Noah's Anna (Great Gramma): The World Through the Eyes of a Child."). I have up to five more in the wings, to be published. However I felt compelled to share this knowledge first. I can honestly say I was guided to write this book.

This is the first self-help book I have written. I hope you can understand and learn you are never too old to change your life. Have faith in God and have faith in your own ability as well.

Remember, once you discover the power of **YOUR** mind; use it for the good and well-being of yourself and others, because 'like attracts like'. That is the law of attraction.

Let me explain it this way. You go to your favourite fast food drive through window, read the menu, place your order, pay at the nest window, pick up a the final window, drive away and enjoy the benefits. You know full well you are getting what you asked for. Life can be that simple, place your order, pay for the order (with your thanks) then receive your order and… enjoy.

Today there is also so much fighting and conflict between countries. I believe the reason for that is because…that is all they are thinking. If they could suddenly change their thoughts to peace and peacefulness, that is what they would have. The reason they fight and kill is they have pinched themselves off from their source. A source that wants us to be happy, abundant and peaceful. This is my source. If my book has only helped one person (perhaps it is you) to learn the power of their mind, then what I have done is worth it for me to have shared with you.

Every time we say 'I am ' we are declaring our divinity. So start saying 'I am, I can, I will'. God as the burning bush said "Moses, Moses", the answer came from Moses "here I am" (Exodus 3:4)

When you get up in the morning, instead of saying "Oh God, it's morning" say instead" Oh God! It's a wonderful morning!"

My life has so changed. I can shop anyplace I want to shop. Go anywhere I want to go. Live in a house I want to live in. This is all up to you. It is in the power of the mind… your mind. If our children were taught this in school, and at home, if our houses of worship would also teach this, it would be a much better world. We could all enjoy our world and its beauty much much better, I often sit by my window looking outside and pondering what life could have been like, if only someone had told me years ago, what it has taken me over 20 years to learn. Perhaps, if my mother had of been taught this…how different things could have been for me.

I tried different houses of worship only to find out they don't know this either. I guess you can't expect them to teach what they do not know. I can say I learned a lot form the book and DVD ' The Secret', while it is excellent, it didn't seem to go deep enough into the mind, at least not for me, to learn this. What we have to learn is to see things the way we want to see them, and not what we think they are.

This is what I learned from reading, I want to share with you, to help you get to where you want to be and not take 20 years to do it. What have you got to lose? Better yet, what you have got to gain!

The truth is, if you think you can or think you cannot, either way you are right.

We all have in our heads the most powerful computer that was ever created. We must learn how to use it correctly to be successful in this life.

The Great Master said "(Give and it will be given to you. They will pour into your lap a good measure—pressed down, shaken together and running over. For by your standard of measure it will be measured to you in return." (Luke 6:38)

So if you give good thoughts to your subconscious mind, they will be shaken together and running over.

The truth of it all is you can overcome any obstacles in your life if you have a mind to. I know, I did it, and against all odds. Never say "I can't". You should only have one goal in your life and that one goal is to feel good no matter what! You should never have to worry about anything else. All your desires should automatically come to you.

I am going to leave you with a secret I learned. If you can think peace in your mind, peace is what you will get. Not only for yourself; but for our planet as well. It is my belief that we all want peace.

I hope you have enjoyed reading this book, and share in what I have learned. I wish you all the best…most of all…I wish you peace.

It is hard to have peace if you are broke and cannot pay your bills. The master Jesus said "the peace that passeth all understanding" (Philippians 4:7) it can be yours and mine.

Remember what the master Jesus said 'and a little child shall lead them.' (Isaiah 11:6)

May all the Noah's of the world start leading us. Yes, you may fall, but pick yourself up, dust yourself off and start all over again, start creating your own life.

This is Noah's mantra,

I am,

I can,

I will,

because

I am number one,

I am a winner,

I am a good boy,

and I have healing hands!!

Thank you for allowing me to share what I have learned through my readings.

May God bless you all!
I wish you great prosperity.

Dorothy

I thought I would share some of my poems I have published in my three poetry books titled

A Book of Children's Poems
By Noah's Anna (Great Gramma):
The World Through the Eyes of a Child."

The poetry books are dedicated to
my two Great-Grandsons

Noah Mangelsen
&
Hayden Mangelsen

And to my family,

Sons Gary, Richard, Darin

Daughters Sylvia, Heather.

Special thanks to my grandsons Rob and Randy for my special inspirations…Hayden and Noah,

(thank you daddies)

Dorothy Mangelsen

I hope you get as much joy out of reading them as I did in writing them.

Summer is Almost Over

Summer is almost over
Fall will soon be here
Leaves will soon be falling
Off the trees so far and near.

The flowers will soon be going to sleep
And winter will soon arrive.
Soon snow will cover the ground
And not a flower will be found.

Spring, summer, and fall
Sleep through the winter months you see.
But when winter leaves, seasons come again
With all their beauty for us to see.

Child at Play

While cleaning up my yard today
I saw a little child at play.

His face was so bright and shinny
In the light of day.

Oh…to be a child again
And only have to play.

Dream Boat

I am a little dream boat
Come along and dream with me,
Bring your precious dreams
And we will see what we can see.

I'll take you out to sea,
Where you a pirate can be,
Or we can go to the islands
Where you can surf with me.

We can sail down the rainbow
And find the 'pot of gold'
Or we can go over the rainbow
To a fairyland I am told.

By now you know your precious dreams
Are in your mind you see.
And I am just a little boat
That's in your memory.

Birdies Birdies

Birdies, birdies,
Sitting in a tree
Chirping and singing,
So happily.

If we could only be,
As happy as thee.
What a wonderful world
It would be.

Three Baby birds

Three little birdies
Sitting in a nest
I wonder if there is one
The mother likes the best.

She cares for them and feeds them
And keeps them warm at night,
Soon she will teach them how to fly
And they will all take flight.

Soon they will make their own nests
And not return, you see
They will care for their own babies
Just like she.

Empty Nest

The nest is now empty,
In the basket on my porch
The baby birds have taken flight
They are nowhere in sight

It is sad to see the empty nest
In the basket on my porch
But the baby birds have gone
To join the rest

I am sure they are happy
They left the basket on my porch

I hope next year
Some new ones will come along
And build another nest…
In the basket on my porch

Song Bird

Song bird song bird
Singing so nice.

I am sure you are singing
Only for me.

Keep on singing all my life
Till I close my eyes
From worry and strife.

Little Dreamer

Dream little dreamer…Dream on
Dream away cares
Dream away fears
Dream little dreamer
Dream on.

Dream of fairies
Sugar and spice,
Dream about everything nice
Dream little dreamer
Dream on.

Guardian Angel

I am your guardian angel,
Though, you think you cannot see me.
I'm in the stars that shine so bright,
The moon, and sunshine too.

The flowers and trees,
And bushes and plants too.
Even in the tiniest things,
I'm there watching you.

If you ever need a friend,
Just call on me, my dear.
Because, I am your guardian angel,
I am always near.

Mugwump

When I was a little baby
I had a small stuffed toy,
My Anna called it Mugwump
And oh! It brought such joy

Anna played peek-a-boo
With me and Mugwump too,
I would laugh, and laugh,
And, Anna had fun too

But now those days are over,
We play other things you see.
Because I am much older…
You see I'll soon be three

Dedicated to my great-grandson Noah
Love, Anna

Basket On My Porch

I have a pretty basket
Hanging on my porch
There are flowers in my basket
Hanging on my porch

A robin came along and built a nest
In the basket on my porch,
There she sits on her nest
In the basket on my porch

The basket sways to and fro
And sooths the mother robin, and her babies so
I love to watch her sitting
In the basket on my porch.

Cloe

I have a cat named Cloe
She likes to sleep in a basket.
Even though she is a little chubby,
To be sleeping in a basket.

She rolls herself up kind of small
To fit inside the basket.
She doesn't care how the basket feels
She doesn't even ask it.

Hayden

Twinkling stars so high above,
Tell me of the angels love,
You shine so high up in the sky,
I sometimes wonder really why.
I cannot touch you as you fly,
Across the sky, so far and wide.

The angels love is in your sparkling eyes,
You shine so bright from up above,
Are you showing me the angels love?
Michael, you protect me,
Peter, you guide me.

The angels come from up above,
And show me Gods love, love, love,
The angels fly around me,
They always will surround me,
With love and gentle tenderness,
They always will protect me.

Though still, still, still you are in the night,
I am never out of your site,
As I slumber in, my little bed,
You are dancing all around my sweet, sweet head.
So always stay here by my side,
And bring the angels far and wide,
Thank you God for stars and angels

Dedicated to my great grandson Hayden
With Love, Great gramma

Why

Why, oh, why
Do dogs bark?
Birds sing?
Cat's meow?

Why, oh, why, does everything
Do the things they do?
Flowers grow
Sun shines
Rain falls from up above

Tell me then why, oh why, oh why
Do people worry and cry,
Instead of showing love?
Can someone tell me why?

Dream Builders

I am a little dream builder
I live high up in the sky,
But when you go to bed at night,
I am always nearby.

I bring you dreams of flowers birds and bees,
I only bring you dreams
Of happiness…you see
So when you go to bed at night
Think of the dream builder…me

Mourning Dove

I love to hear the mourning doves
As they coo so soft and low,
They are a very docile bird you know.

They feed on mostly sun flower seeds
And pick them off the ground.
I have to wonder…

Maybe
That is where
They get their sweet
Soft cooing sound.

Playing in the Puddles

I love to play in the puddles on the ground
I sometimes wish they would stay all year round
But when winter comes, and snow covers the ground
There are no more puddles around

But at last when winter leaves
And spring time rolls around
Once again I can play
In the puddles on the ground

Rain Drop

I am a little rain drop
Falling from the sky
I come from up above
Way up so very high.

Alone, I can do nothing
But with so many other raindrops
I keep the ground from getting dry.

Everything that grows needs water
Including you and I
Always remember that water
Comes from way up, in the sky.

Happy Little Brook

I like to go and sit beside
A happy little brook
I sit and watch the water
Or sometimes read a book.

The woods are oh so quiet
It's a lovely time of day
Oh what a beautiful time
To just sit and pray

When the day is over
And the sun is going down
I pick up my bag of dreams
And head back into town.

Sunflower

I am a pretty sunflower
I grow so tall and straight,
I turn my face up to the sun
From morn…till day is done.

My colour is bright yellow,
(I am a happy fellow)
So when you plant my seeds;
Make sure I'm in a place
Where the sun can shine on my face
That is why they call me…..A SUNFLOWER!

Angels Watching

The stars that shine so bright at night
are Angels watching me.
I feel so safe all through the night,
when the Angels are watching me

They hover all around my head
as I sleep so peacefully…
because
I know the angels
are taking care of me.

Popping Seeds

Greens are popping
Through the ground,
Little seedlings
Can be found.

They never make a sound
But still they pop through the ground.
Springtime is on the way,
You see it more every day.

Soon the flowers will start to bloom
To end all winter gloom,
So, put a smile on your face,
Look up to the sun!
Wintertime is done!

Write your own poem here!

Write your own poem here!

Write your own poem here!

Write your own poem here!

www.ingramcontent.com/pod-product-compliance
Lightning Source LLC
Chambersburg PA
CBHW030135100526
44591CB00009B/672